# Math Thinkercises

by
**Becky Daniel**

**illustrated by Nancee McClure**

Cover by Nancee McClure

Copyright © Good Apple, Inc., 1988

ISBN No. 0-86653-429-6

Printing No. 987654321

**GOOD APPLE, INC.**
**BOX 299**
**CARTHAGE, IL 62321-0299**

# Dedication

This book is dedicated to my daughter, Amy, who thinks figuring out what day of the week Christmas will fall on in the year 2000 is a great way to spend an afternoon. (She says it will be on a Monday.)

# Table of Contents

# To the Teacher

*Math Thinkercises* is designed to give students' minds a real workout! Children will experience a new understanding of mathematics when they tackle these exciting and motivating puzzles. The wide range of activities, from simple to complex, gives learners concrete practice in finding patterns, numeration, permutation and problem solving.

Unfortunately, most school-aged children are involved in math programs based on memorizing math facts rather than higher thinking mathematical reasoning. The activities in this book require children to apply rules, methods, principles and theories to new materials. The complexity of most of the activities make the use of calculators acceptable and even a necessity. Encourage students to discuss solutions with classmates, parents and other adults. Working in a group with a given time limit is another good way to use the activities in this book. Remember, the thinking process is more important than finding the solution, but don't deny children the satisfaction of arriving at an acceptable answer.

Each page contains a bonus. These activities are usually very difficult and should not be a requirement. Use these activities for extra credit. Students that complete one of these should receive special recognition. A class competition could involve keeping track of how many bonuses are completed by each student and rewarding those that complete a given number. Awards are found on pages 59 and 60, and a special award certificate for bonuses is included.

An answer key is provided; however, since sometimes there are several acceptable answers, the answer key will only provide a list of possible answers. For many math activity pages, learners will have their own unique answers. Discussion of alternative answers and the steps involved in reaching answers should be encouraged. If time allows, have the children follow up each activity page by creating their own puzzles.

# Number Patterns

Study the numbers in each row. Look for a pattern. When you think you know the pattern, figure out what number should come next and write it on the blank that follows each row of numbers.

Example: 2 4 6 8 10 (add 2, repeat)

1. 10 15 13 18 16 21 19 _____

2. 2 4 8 16 20 40 44 88 _____

3. 10 30 32 96 98 294 296 _____

4. 1 5 12 60 67 335 _____

5. 7 8 10 13 17 22 28 35 _____

6. 5 12 18 23 27 30 _____

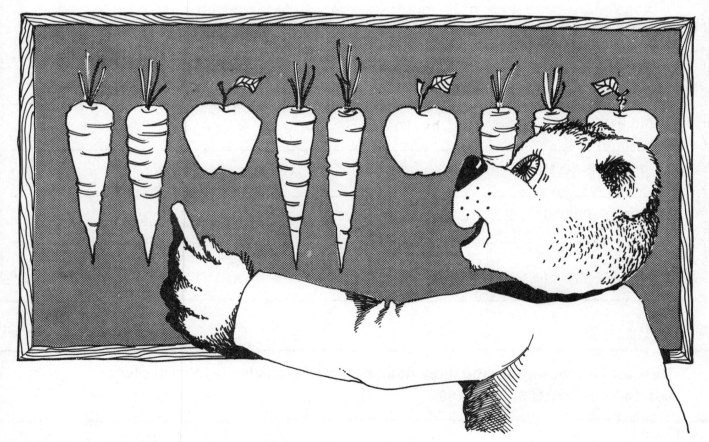

**Bonus:** What number comes next?

6      72      738      7,404

Name _____

1

# Associations

Each of the three number pairs relates to each other in the same way. If you can figure out how they relate, you will know what number is missing in each row. List the association under each problem.

Example: 1:3  3:9  6:18  4:

The second number is always three times the first number.
So the missing number is 12 (4 x 3 = 12).

1. 20:4  15:3  10:2  5:

   _____

2. 2:22  80:100  90:110  110:

   _____

3. 45:9  89:17  68:14  66:

   _____

4. 4:6  8:12  10:15  12:

   _____

5. 501:15  988:89  753:37  821:

   _____

---

**Bonus:** In what way are the three number pairs associated with each other?
961:196        901:106        98:86

Name _____

# A Difficult Arrangement

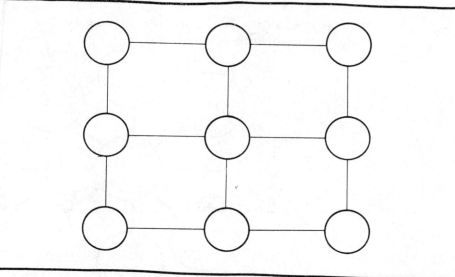

1. Arrange the digits 1-9 in the circles above in such a way that each row across and down has the same total. Hint: Each row will total 15.

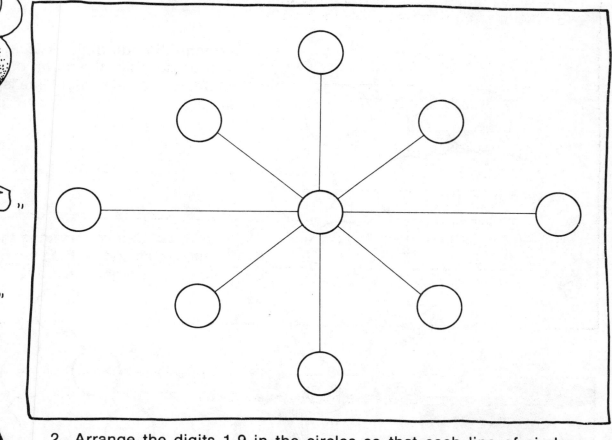

2. Arrange the digits 1-9 in the circles so that each line of circles connected by a line has the same total. Hint: The number 5 should be placed in the center circle.

**Bonus:** Can you arrange the digits 1 through 9 in two rows whose sums are equal?

Name _____

# Magic Circles

1. Arrange the digits 10-18 in the circles so that the sum of the numbers in each straight line is the same.

2. Arrange the odd digits 9-25 in the circles so that the sum of the numbers in each straight line is the same.

**Bonus:** Can you arrange the digits 1-9 in the circles so that the sum of the numbers in each straight line is 17?

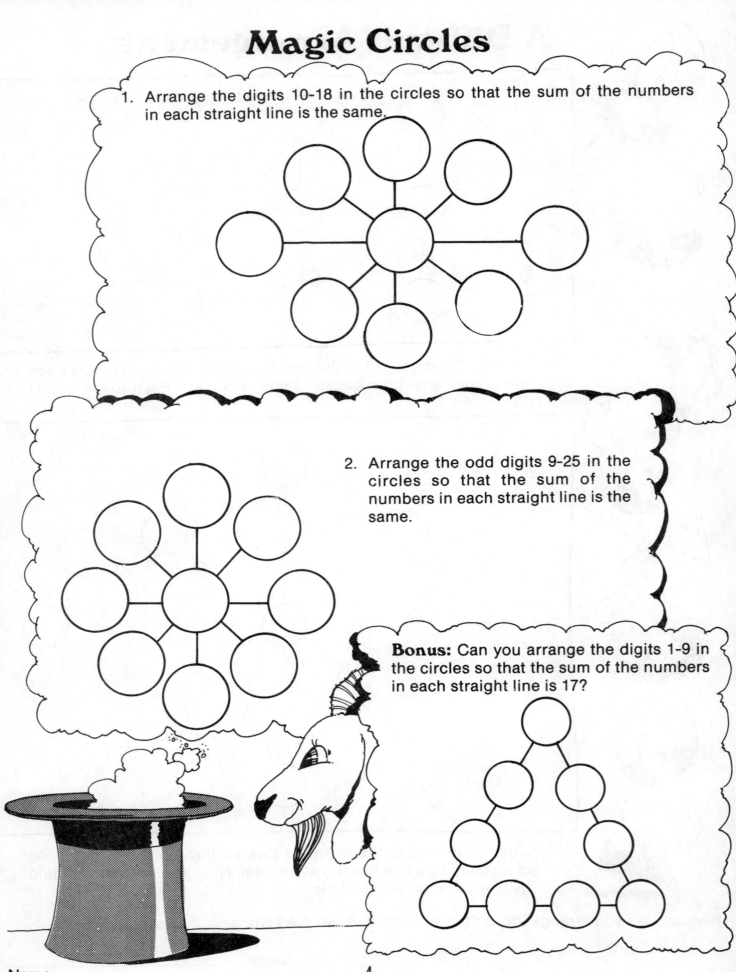

Name _____

4

# Magic Triangles

1. Arrange the digits 1-6 in the circles so that the sum of the numbers in each straight line is the same.

2. Arrange the digits 7-12 in the circles so that the sum of the numbers in each straight line is the same.

**Bonus:** Can you arrange the digits 1-9 in the circles so that the sum of the numbers in each straight line is equal?

Name _____

# Magic Stars

1. Arrange the five digits 12, 14, 15, 16 and 18 in the circles so that the sum of the numbers in each straight line is 36. Some of the numbers have been placed to get you started.

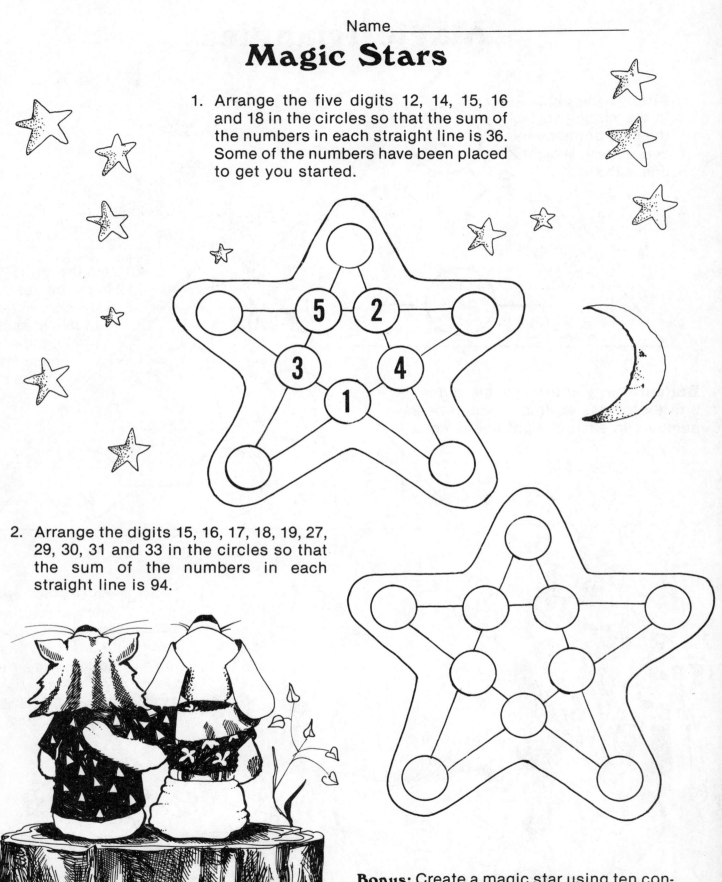

2. Arrange the digits 15, 16, 17, 18, 19, 27, 29, 30, 31 and 33 in the circles so that the sum of the numbers in each straight line is 94.

**Bonus:** Create a magic star using ten consecutive odd digits of your choice.

# Magic Squares

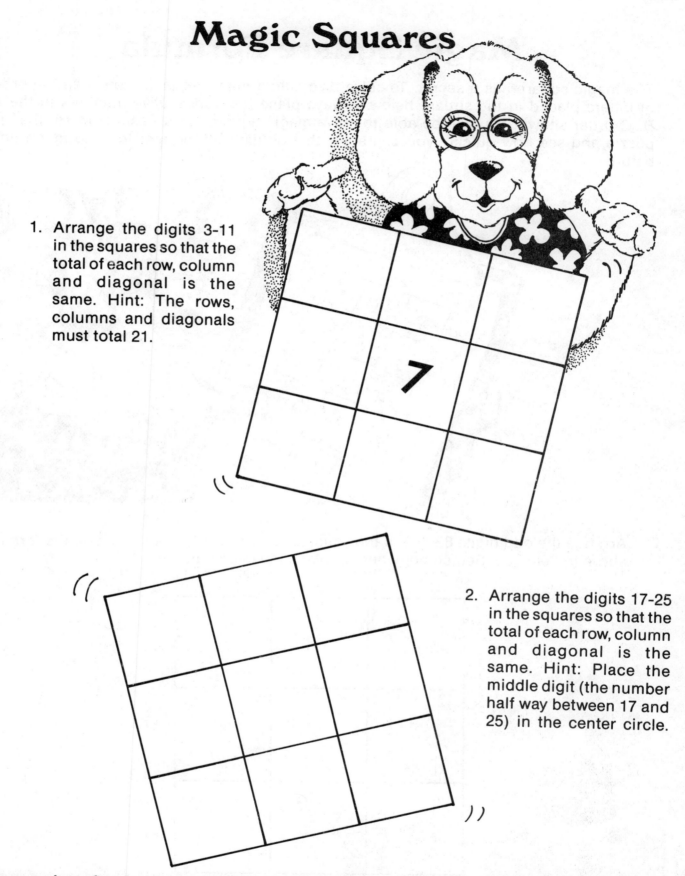

1. Arrange the digits 3-11 in the squares so that the total of each row, column and diagonal is the same. Hint: The rows, columns and diagonals must total 21.

2. Arrange the digits 17-25 in the squares so that the total of each row, column and diagonal is the same. Hint: Place the middle digit (the number half way between 17 and 25) in the center circle.

**Bonus:** A perfect square is a number formed by multiplying a whole number by itself. 9 is a perfect square (3 x 3 = 9). What perfect square can be turned upside down and still be a perfect square?

Name _____

# Magic Square Formula

The magic square has a secret. To solve or create a magic square, memorize the order of letters placed in the square below. Always place the consecutive numbers in the A, B, C order shown. You will be able to solve magic squares in a flash! Now try the last puzzle and see how quickly you can solve this difficult puzzle that took so much time before.

f a h
g e c
b i d

a = first number
b = second number
c = third number
etc.

1. Arrange the odd digits 89-105 in the squares to form a magic square. Use the formula above to help you. Remember where to place the middle number.

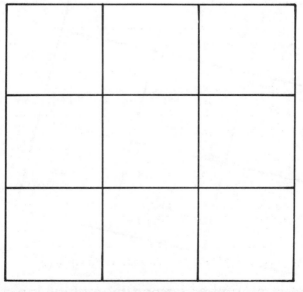

**Bonus:** Two mothers and two daughters divide thirty-one dollar bills evenly among them. How much did each person get?

Name _____

# I See Spots

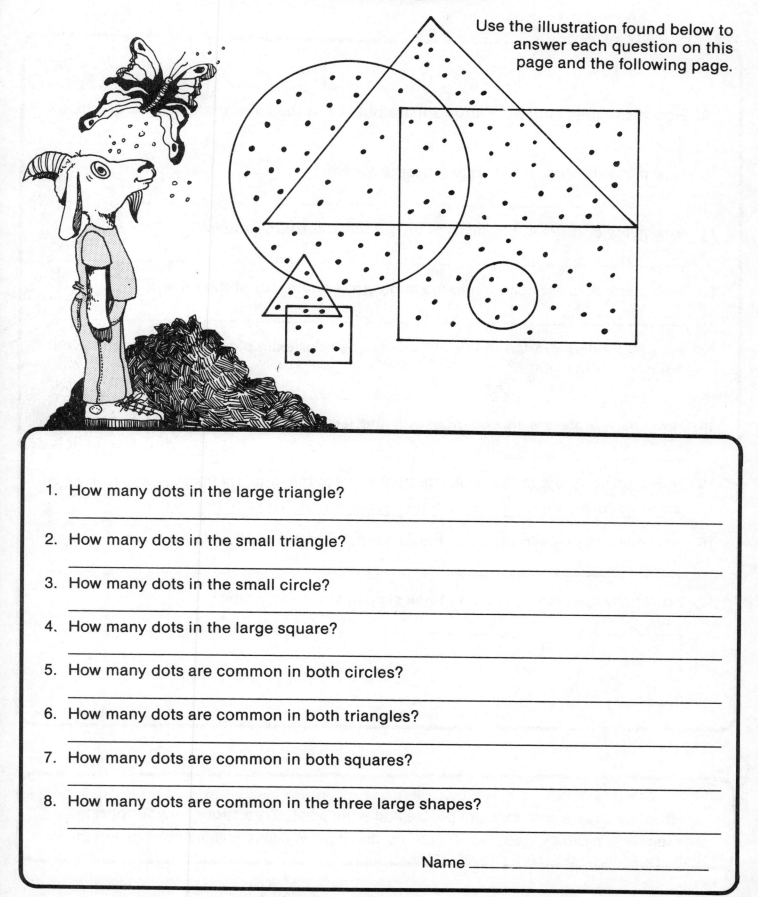

Use the illustration found below to answer each question on this page and the following page.

1. How many dots in the large triangle?
   _____

2. How many dots in the small triangle?
   _____

3. How many dots in the small circle?
   _____

4. How many dots in the large square?
   _____

5. How many dots are common in both circles?
   _____

6. How many dots are common in both triangles?
   _____

7. How many dots are common in both squares?
   _____

8. How many dots are common in the three large shapes?
   _____

Name _____

# I See Spots (cont'd.)

9. How many dots are in the large square but not in the large triangle or large circle?

_____

10. How many dots are common to the large shapes?

_____

11. How many dots are in the small circle but not in the large square?

_____

12. How many dots are common to the large circle and either of the triangles?

_____

13. How many dots are found in only one shape? For example, dots in the square but not in any other shape?

_____

14. How many dots are in common with the large square and either of the circles?

_____

15. How many dots are in the large square but not in the large triangle?

_____

16. How many dots are in the small triangle but not in the small square?

_____

17. How many dots are common to three shapes at the same time?

_____

**Bonus:** Create your own dot puzzle and write a list of questions for your puzzle.

Name _____

# Cut the Pies

1. Draw five lines across the circle. What is the most pieces that the "pie" can be divided into with five lines? Twelve? Fourteen?

2. Draw six lines across the circle. What is the most pieces that the circle can be divided into with six lines? Twelve? Fourteen? Sixteen? Eighteen?

**Bonus:** Divide 100 by ½, add 16, subtract 19. What is your answer?

Name _____

# Ring Just Three

1. Find and circle ten combinations of three digits that total 9. The three numbers must touch edges as shown in the example. Every number must be used only once.

```
6   9   0   0   8
2   1   4   0   1
2   1   4   3   7
2   6   4   2   1
5   3   0   5   1
8   0   1   3   1
```

2. Find and circle ten combinations of three digits that total a mystery sum. The three numbers must touch edges as in the last puzzle. All the numbers will be circled when the puzzle is complete.

```
9   6   6   3   7
1   5   8   7   1
9   3   7   4   8
3   7   0   9   3
6   8   0   3   3
3   6   9   3   3
```

Mystery sum is _____

**Bonus:** Rearrange the circles so that there are four circles in the bottom row, three circles in the next to the bottom row, two in the next to the top row and one circle in the top row. You must move only three circles.

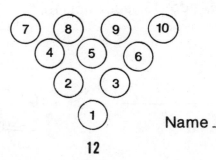

Name _____

# Fractions

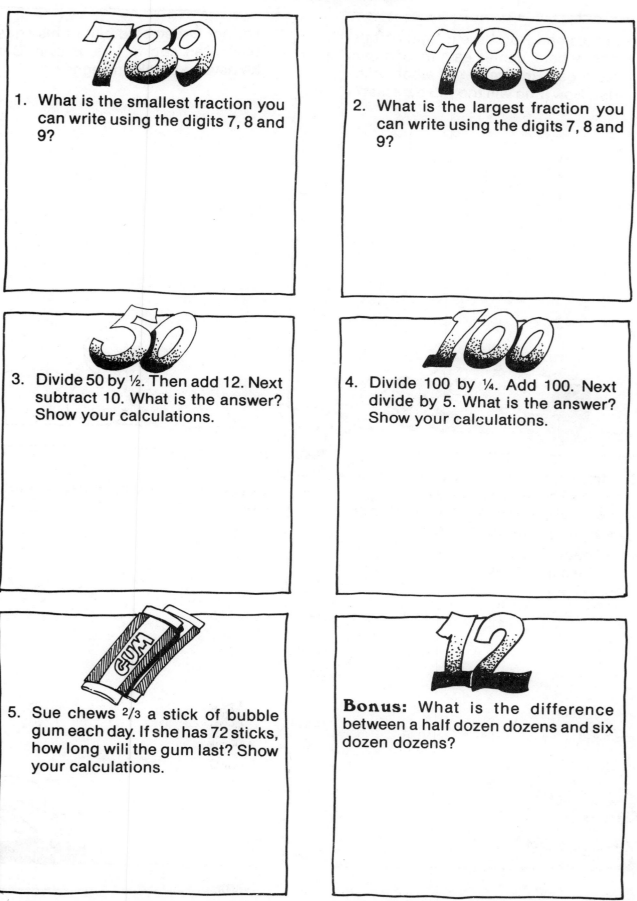

1. What is the smallest fraction you can write using the digits 7, 8 and 9?

2. What is the largest fraction you can write using the digits 7, 8 and 9?

3. Divide 50 by ½. Then add 12. Next subtract 10. What is the answer? Show your calculations.

4. Divide 100 by ¼. Add 100. Next divide by 5. What is the answer? Show your calculations.

5. Sue chews ²/₃ a stick of bubble gum each day. If she has 72 sticks, how long will the gum last? Show your calculations.

**Bonus:** What is the difference between a half dozen dozens and six dozen dozens?

Name _____

# More Fractions

1. James and Ron have a total of 143 candy bars. James eats $\frac{1}{3}$ of a bar each day. Ron eats ¾ of a bar each day. How long will the 143 bars last?

2. Farmer Green sold half of his eggs plus ½ an egg to Mrs. Brown. Did he have to break any eggs?

3. Mrs. Peters has eight boys and no girls. The Peters are expecting a new baby soon. What are the odds that they will get a girl this time?

   a. better than 50%
   b. less than 50%
   c. 50%

**Bonus:** What is a third and a half of a third of 12?

Name _____

# A Question of Time

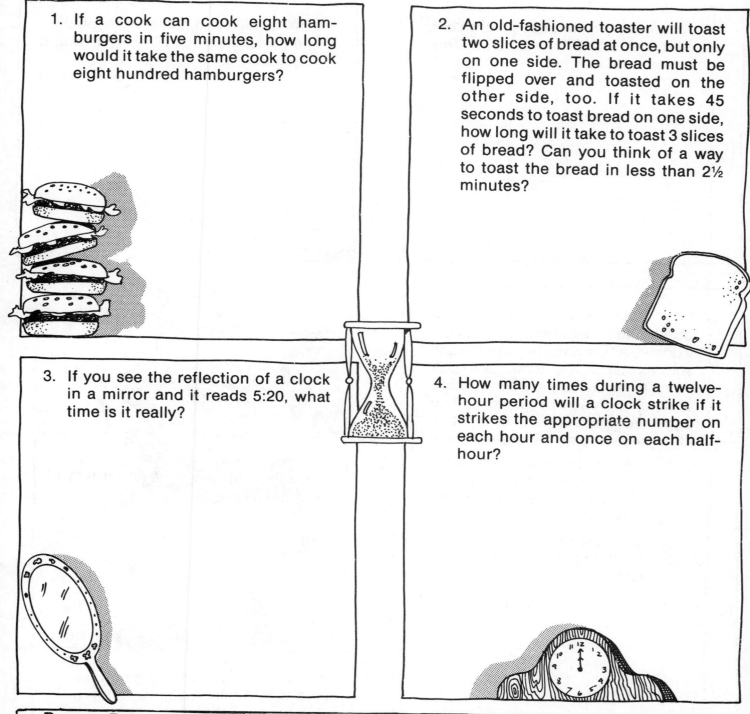

1. If a cook can cook eight hamburgers in five minutes, how long would it take the same cook to cook eight hundred hamburgers?

2. An old-fashioned toaster will toast two slices of bread at once, but only on one side. The bread must be flipped over and toasted on the other side, too. If it takes 45 seconds to toast bread on one side, how long will it take to toast 3 slices of bread? Can you think of a way to toast the bread in less than 2½ minutes?

3. If you see the reflection of a clock in a mirror and it reads 5:20, what time is it really?

4. How many times during a twelve-hour period will a clock strike if it strikes the appropriate number on each hour and once on each half-hour?

**Bonus:** Roberta's watch is five minutes slow and she thinks it's ten minutes fast. Suzi's watch is five minutes fast and she thinks it is five minutes slow. Fern's watch is ten minutes fast and she thinks it's ten minutes slow. Each plans to leave for school when she thinks it is 8:55. The bell rings at 9:00. If the walk to school is four minutes, who will be late for school?

Name _____

# Money Problems

1. Jim gave the shopkeeper six coins that totaled 38¢ for a balloon. What were the six coins?

2. What bills and coins are needed to make exactly $57.03 with 7 bills and 8 coins?

3. Mrs. Brown sold eggs for 50¢ a dozen and little green apples for 30¢ a dozen. At the Saturday Market she sold a total of 120 items. She took home three one dollar bills, one half dollar and three dimes. How many eggs did she sell and how many little green apples did she sell?

**Bonus:** A boy paid $59 for a bike. He paid with 4 bills. What were the bills?

Name _____

# More Money Problems

1. At the candy shop you can buy two peppermint patties and a lollipop for the same amount as you can buy two gumdrops and one peppermint patty. You can buy one of each for 9¢. If gumdrops cost 1¢ less than peppermint patties and 1¢ more than lollipops, how much does each kind of candy cost?

2. Michelle wants to buy a telescope that costs $300.00. She has saved half the amount she needs. She gets a $3.00 allowance each week. Will it take more or less than a year to save for the telescope?

3. Sam works at the car wash. On Monday he earned a certain amount of money. On Tuesday he earned twice as much as he did on Monday. On Wednesday he earned half as much as he did on Monday. The three days' total earnings was $70.00. How much did he earn on each day?

**Bonus:** Can you think of a combination of 100 coins that totals $5? Can you think of two combinations that total $5?

Name_____

# Cross All Ways

Can you place an X in five of the squares so that there is one and only one X in each row, column and main diagonals?

**Bonus:** Draw an 8 x 8 square. It will contain 64 squares. Put an X in 8 of the 64 squares so that there is one and only one X in each row, column and main diagonals?

Name _____

# Pure Magic Squares

A magic square is an arrangement of digits in a square such that the sums of the digits in each row, column and main diagonal are always equal to the same number. The magic squares found on this page and the following page are pure magic squares. The digits used in each puzzle are consecutive.

1. Complete this magic square using the consecutive digits 1-9. The total for each row, column and main diagonal is 15. Some of the digits have been placed to help you get started.

| 6 |   |   |
|---|---|---|
|   | 5 |   |
|   | 9 | 4 |

2. Complete this magic square using the consecutive digits 7-15. The total for each row, column and main diagonal is 33. Some of the digits have been placed to help you get started.

| 12 | 7 |    |
|----|---|----|
|    | 11|    |
|    |   | 10 |

**Bonus:** Which weighs more, a pound of gold or a pound of feathers?

Name _____

# More Pure Magic Squares

Name_____

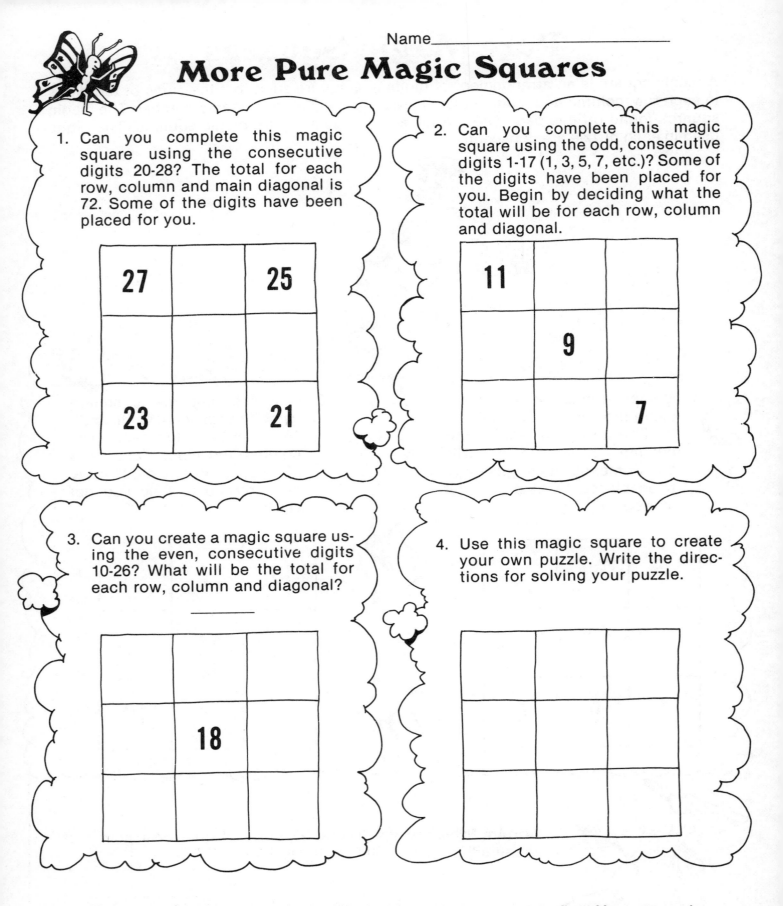

1. Can you complete this magic square using the consecutive digits 20-28? The total for each row, column and main diagonal is 72. Some of the digits have been placed for you.

| 27 |  | 25 |
|----|----|----|
|  |  |  |
| 23 |  | 21 |

2. Can you complete this magic square using the odd, consecutive digits 1-17 (1, 3, 5, 7, etc.)? Some of the digits have been placed for you. Begin by deciding what the total will be for each row, column and diagonal.

| 11 |  |  |
|----|----|----|
|  | 9 |  |
|  |  | 7 |

3. Can you create a magic square using the even, consecutive digits 10-26? What will be the total for each row, column and diagonal?

_____

|  |  |  |
|----|----|----|
|  | 18 |  |
|  |  |  |

4. Use this magic square to create your own puzzle. Write the directions for solving your puzzle.

|  |  |  |
|----|----|----|
|  |  |  |
|  |  |  |

**Bonus:** Arrange six pencils so that each touches the other five. You may not break or bend any of the pencils.

20

# Mathematical Codes

Name _____

Put the consecutive digits 1-9 in the spaces so that the number sentences are true. Example: ☐ + ☐ = ⌋ or 2 + 2 = 4

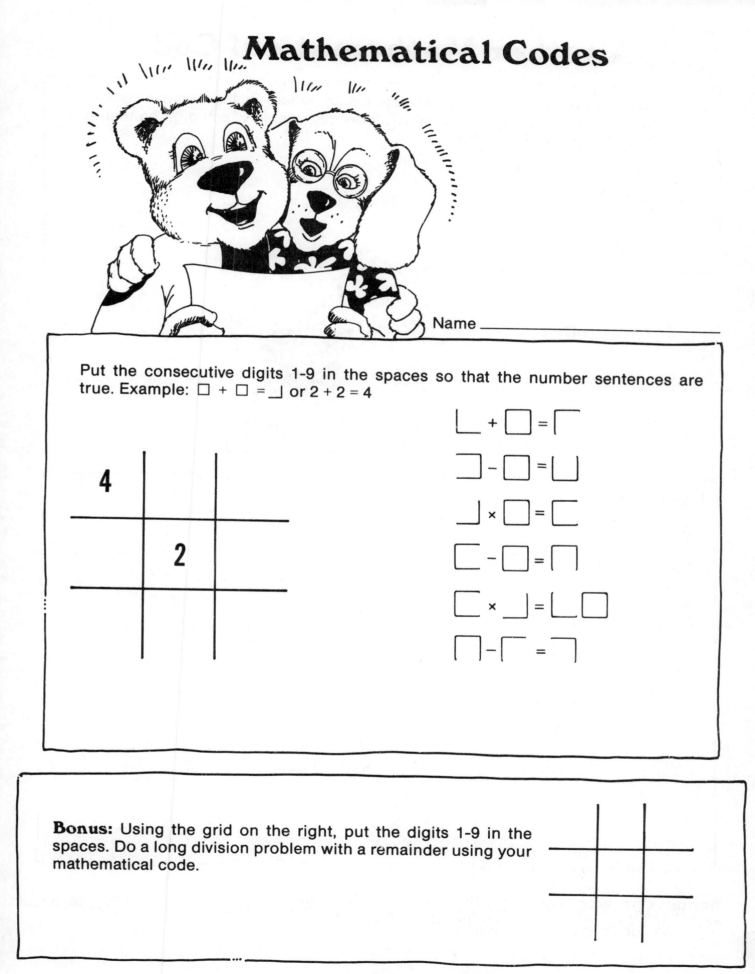

**Bonus:** Using the grid on the right, put the digits 1-9 in the spaces. Do a long division problem with a remainder using your mathematical code.

# Another Mathematical Code

The consecutive digits 0-5 are represented by letters in the number sentences found below. Can you figure out which letter represents which digit so that each number sentence will be true?

$G + G = G$
$D + D = FG$
$F + F = A$
$A + A = B$
$F + A = E$

Figure here.

$0 = G$
$1 = F$
$2 = A$
$3 = E$
$4 = B$
$5 = D$

**Bonus:** Give each digit 0-9 a letter symbol. Then see if you can spell words that equal each other. Example: s = 1, e = 2, m = 3    SEE = ME

# Word Problems

1. Nannette, Jay and Brad have a total of 80 pieces of bubble gum. The total number of pieces that Nannette and Brad have equals the number of pieces that Jay has. Jay has four times as many as Brad. How many pieces of gum does each child have?

Nannette?
Brad?
Jay?

2. Ralph read a book with more than 100 pages and less than 200 pages. The total of the three digits is 10. The second digit is twice the last digit. How many pages did Ralph's book have?

3. Three children collect marbles. Martha has twice as many as Wally. The three children have a total of 1,454 marbles. If Joe had one more marble, he would have 210 marbles. How many marbles does each child have?

Martha?
Wally?
Joe?

4. Ruth has three red hens, six speckled hens, one white hen and seven black hens. How many of the hens can say they are the same color as another hen?

**Bonus:** If a golf ball is dropped from a 100-foot building, assuming it rebounds half the distance it falls, how far will the ball travel by the time it hits the ground the fourth time?

Name _____

# More Word Problems

1. When Brenda did her arithmetic, she accidentally confused two digits. In the problems below you will find incorrect answers. If you reverse two digits, all the number sentences will be true. Which two digits are reversed? Rewrite each problem correctly.

   62 + 50 = 132
   77 + 26 = 81
   5 + 5 = 14
   66 + 21 = 85

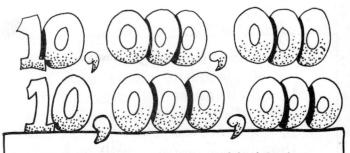

4. What number can be added to ten million and get a total that is ten million more than if you multiplied ten million by the same digit?

2. If Henry has 1,490 baseball cards in one stack, 1,887 baseball cards in another stack and 1,000 baseball cards in three other stacks and he places the stacks together, how many stacks will he have?

3. What digit can you add to ten million and get more than if you multiplied the same number by ten million?

5. If you roll one die and get a six, five times in a row, what are the chances of rolling another six the next time you roll the die?

   a. very good chance, since you are rolling a winning streak

   b. very small chance after rolling a six that many times before

   c. one chance in six

**Bonus:** Tom has 66 marbles. If there are twice as many orange as greens, one less blue than green, and seven more reds than greens, how many of each color marbles does Tom have?

Name _____

# Mathematical Sentences

Substitute the correct digits 0-9 for the letters in each puzzle and the math sentences will be correct.

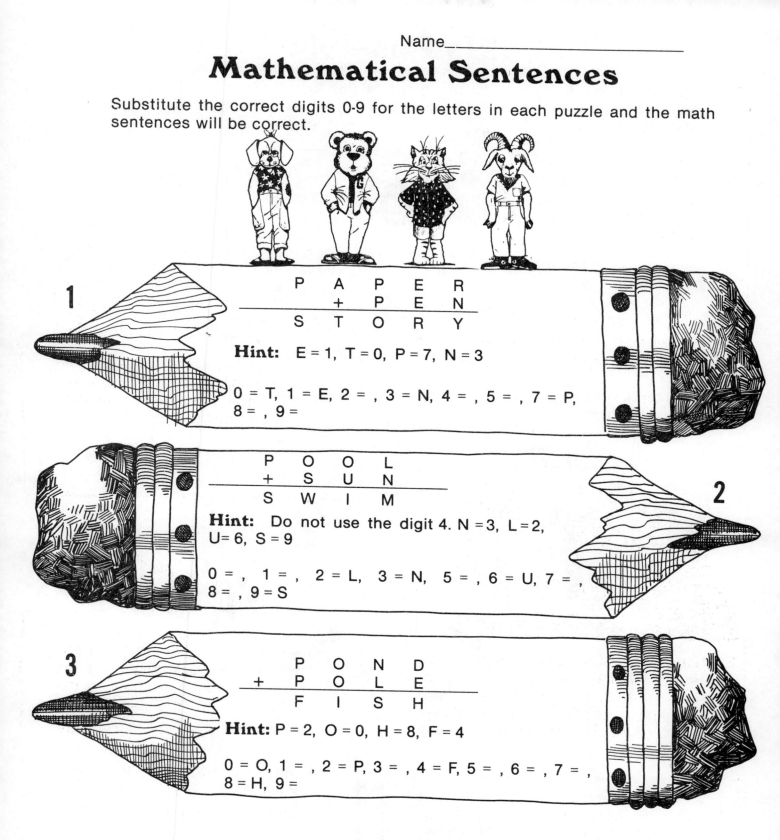

**1**

```
  P A P E R
+   P E N
---------
  S T O R Y
```

**Hint:** E = 1, T = 0, P = 7, N = 3

0 = T, 1 = E, 2 = ___ , 3 = N, 4 = ___ , 5 = ___ , 7 = P,
8 = ___ , 9 = ___

**2**

```
  P O O L
+ S U N
---------
S W I M
```

**Hint:** Do not use the digit 4. N = 3, L = 2,
U = 6, S = 9

0 = ___ , 1 = ___ , 2 = L, 3 = N, 5 = ___ , 6 = U, 7 = ___ ,
8 = ___ , 9 = S

**3**

```
  P O N D
+ P O L E
---------
  F I S H
```

**Hint:** P = 2, O = 0, H = 8, F = 4

0 = O, 1 = ___ , 2 = P, 3 = ___ , 4 = F, 5 = ___ , 6 = ___ , 7 = ___ ,
8 = H, 9 = ___

**Bonus:** One night a man named Jack went to bed at 10:00, but he couldn't sleep. His digital clock was sitting on the nightstand upside down. He noticed that some of the numbers looked like letters. If 1 = i, 3 = e, 4 = h, 5 = s, 7 = l and 0 = o, how many words did he read on his clock before he finally fell asleep at 3:45? What were the words?

# It Is Possible

1. Circle only three digits in the box that total 26. You may have to think to solve this one, but once you discover the secret, it will be as easy as standing on your head.

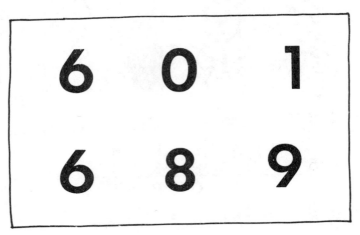

2. Circle only three digits in the box that total 11.

**Bonus:** What is the difference between twice twenty-two and twice two and twenty?

Name _____

# Where's the Sign?

Add only one arithmetic sign to make each mathematical sentence true.

1. 7 8 9 3 6 = 7 5 3

2. 7 2 4 9 1 = 8 1 5

3. 6 3 2 4 3 = 1 8 9 7 2

4. 5 0 9 1 8 9 = 5 1 8 0

5. 5 6 8 3 4 = 1 9 3 1 2

6. 7 0 7 0 7 = 1 0 1 0

7. 9 3 4 4 6 3 = 4 3 2 4 4 2

8. 7 0 4 3 8 4 = 6 9 5 9

9. 6 0 2 1 3 = 1 8 0 6 3

10. 4 5 2 1 3 1 = 4 4 9 0

**Bonus:** Place ten pennies in a row on a table. Stack them in piles of two by jumping over exactly two coins in each move. Write your solution here.

# Signing Off

Add only one mathematical sign to make each math sentence true.

1. 701    52 = 36452

2. 8 9 3 4 6 = 1 4 8 9

3. 4 3 6 5 3 = 1 3 0 9 5

4. 1 4 5 2 2 0 = 2 9 0 4 0

5. 1 2 3 4 2 6 = 2 0 5 7

6. 5 8 2 0 5 = 1 1 6 4

**Bonus:** What three digits added or multiplied by each other equal the same answer?

Name _____

# Double Trouble

Place two signs, one of which will always be an equal sign, in each row of numbers to make mathematical problems followed by their answers.

Example:  6  1  5  3  0  5

$$61 \times 5 = 305$$

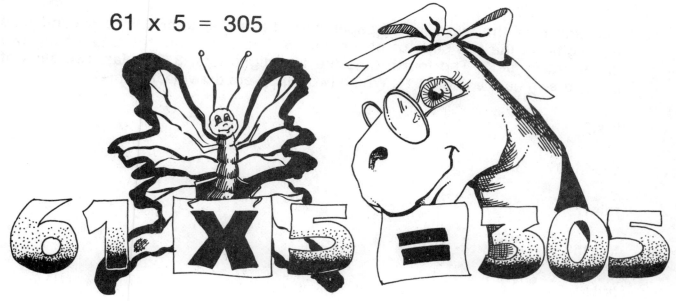

1. 7 2 8 0 1 5 2

2. 9 3 3 3 1

3. 9 5 9 0 5

4. 8 1 0 1 1 7 9 9

5. 8 9 4 6 1 4 9

6. 9 7 8 3 2 0 9 8 0 3

**Bonus:** How many 7's are there between 1 and 100?

Name _____

# Slip, Please

The digits 0-9 are written on separate slips of paper and placed in a hat. Five times, two slips are drawn out. Use the clues found below to figure out which two numbers are drawn out each of the five times.

The first time the two slips of paper have digits that total 9. The second time the digits on the two slips of paper total 5. The third time the total of the two digits drawn is 12. The fourth time the two digits total 8. The last two slips of paper drawn have a total of 11. Which two slips were drawn each time?

first?

second?

third?

fourth?

fifth?

**Bonus:** How many different two-digit numbers can be written with the digits 1-9?

Name _____

# Think First

Can you write the figures for the numbers listed below?

1. one thousand one


2. twelve thousand nine hundred and forty-four


3. nine million forty-five


4. eighty-five hundred eighty-five


5. one million, one hundred thousand one


6. six thousand, twelve hundred sixty-six


**Bonus:** How many times can you subtract 30 from 1000?

Name _____

# Big Fives

1. Can you write an equation that has a total of 65, using four 5's and no other digits?

2. Can you write an equation that has a total of 66, using five 5's and no other digits?

3. Can you write an equation that has a total of 57, using six 5's and no other digits?

4. Can you write an equation that has a product of 30,525, using five 5's and no other digits?

5. Can you write an equation that has a quotient of 10,101, using eight 5's and no other digits?

6. Can you write a fraction that will reduce to 111, using four 5's?

**Bonus:** Why will Ireland become the richest country in the world someday?

Name _____

# Lucky 7's

1. Write a number sentence that has a product of 7, using five 7's and no other digits.

2. Write a number sentence that totals 7, using seven 7's and no other digits.

3. Write a number sentence that has a product of 59,829, using six 7's and no other digits.

4. Write a number sentence that has a difference of 700, using five 7's and no other digits.

5. Write a number sentence that has a quotient of 101, using six 7's and no other digits.

6. How many numbers between 1 and 1,000 can be divided by 7 without a remainder?

**Bonus:** What odd number becomes even if its head is chopped off?

Name _____

# Consecutive Numbers

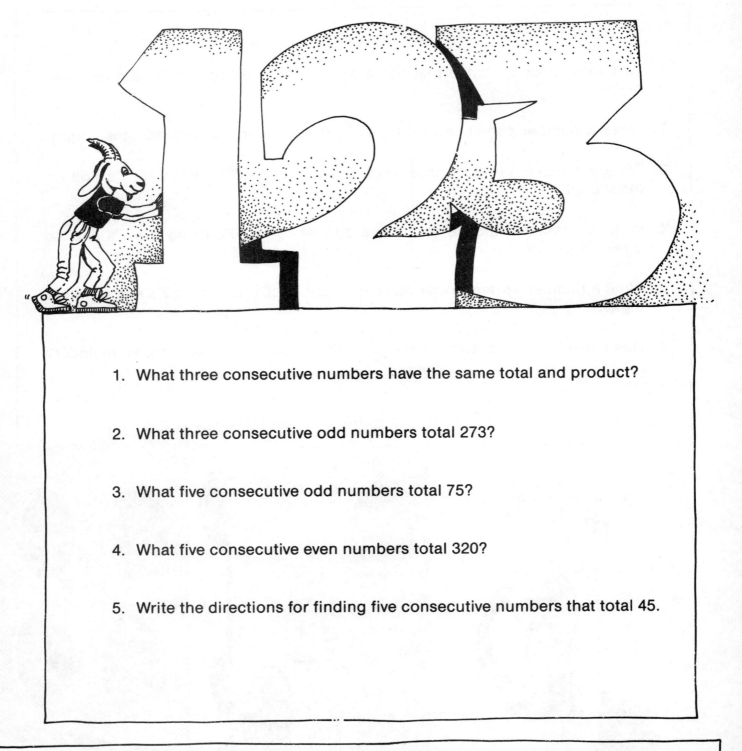

1. What three consecutive numbers have the same total and product?

2. What three consecutive odd numbers total 273?

3. What five consecutive odd numbers total 75?

4. What five consecutive even numbers total 320?

5. Write the directions for finding five consecutive numbers that total 45.

**Bonus:** The same digit placed in each blank will make this problem correct.

```
   7 6 __
 x 5 __
42,07 __
```

Name _____

34

# What Number?

1. What number doubled and then divided by 8 equals 2?

2. Can you write the digit 8 three times and add one line so that it equals 11?

3. What two-digit number is equal to three times the product of its digits?

4. What number multiplied by itself equals 2,401?

5. What two digits have a greater total than product? One of the digits is not zero.

Name _____

**Bonus:** Eric can wash a car in two hours. It takes John three hours to wash the car. Working together, how long will it take Eric and John to wash the car?

# Products

1. What two odd numbers have a product of 141?

2. What two odd numbers have a product of 585?

3. What two odd numbers have a product of 61?

4. What two-digit number plus half its value equals 99?

5. What two-digit number plus twice its value equals 264?

6. What three different odd numbers have a total of 13?

7. What three consecutive odd numbers have a total of 45?

**Bonus:** If a 6'2" barber weighs 330 pounds and a 5'10" teacher weighs 190 pounds, what does a 6' butcher weigh?

Name _____

# Just a Speck

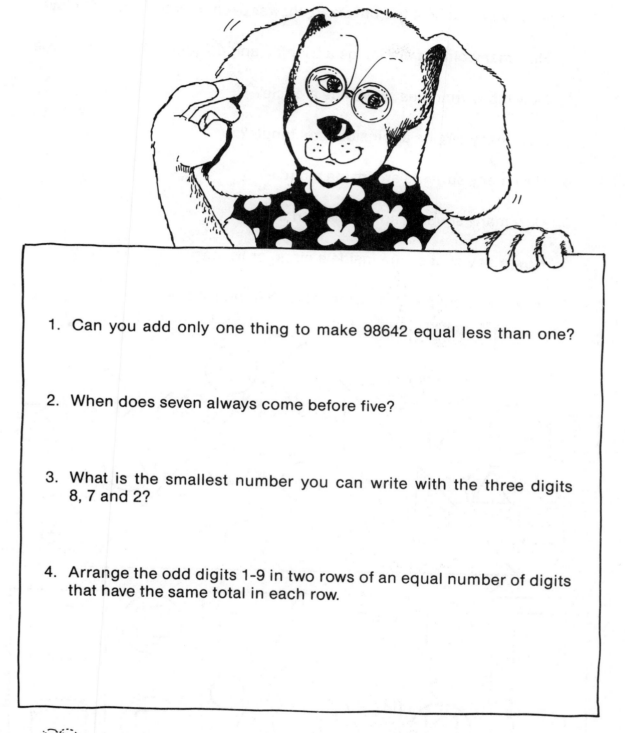

1. Can you add only one thing to make 98642 equal less than one?

2. When does seven always come before five?

3. What is the smallest number you can write with the three digits 8, 7 and 2?

4. Arrange the odd digits 1-9 in two rows of an equal number of digits that have the same total in each row.

**Bonus:** If one cubic foot of dirt has 2,000,000 grains of sand, how many grains of sand in a hole 6' x 4' x 3'?

Name _____

# Puzzle Picture

Look very carefully at the puzzle to answer each question found below.

1. How many circles are inside a triangle and a square at the same time?

2. How many triangles are inside a circle?

3. How many circles are inside a rectangle?

4. How many squares are inside a circle?

5. How many squares are inside a triangle?

6. How many shapes are inside a circle or triangle?

7. How many shapes are inside more than one shape?

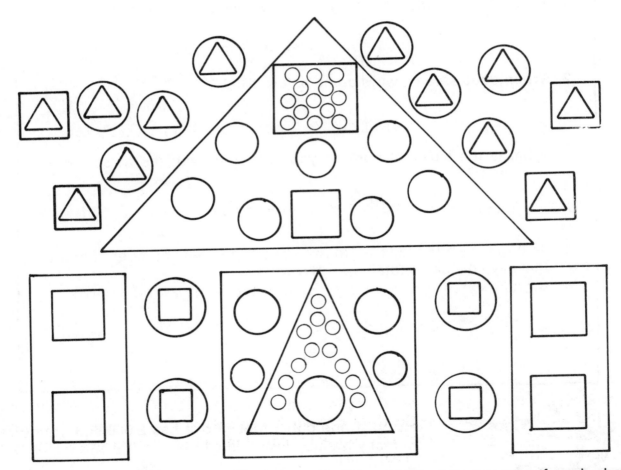

**Bonus:** Draw your own shape-counting puzzle. Keep track of how many of each shape you draw. Write a list of questions for your counting puzzle. Exchange papers with a friend and see who can finish first.

Name _____

# Totals 100

1. Add only one arithmetic sign to five 1's to get the answer, 100.

   1 1 1 1 1 = 100

2. Add only one arithmetic sign to six 3's to get the answer, 110,889.

   3 3 3 3 3 3 = 110,889

3. Add only one arithmetic sign to five 5's to get the answer, 500.

   5 5 5 5 5 = 500

4. Add only one arithmetic sign to six 9's to get the answer, 1998.

   9 9 9 9 9 9 = 1998

5. Add only one arithmetic sign to five 8's to get the answer, 8896.

   8 8 8 8 8 = 8896

**Bonus:** Three sisters received a gift of three dollars, all in dimes. The number of dimes totaled the sum of their ages. So they divided it according to their ages. If Cathy's age is four times Alice's age and Becky is six years older than Alice and six years younger than Cathy, how many dimes did each sister get?

Name _____

# For Experts Only!

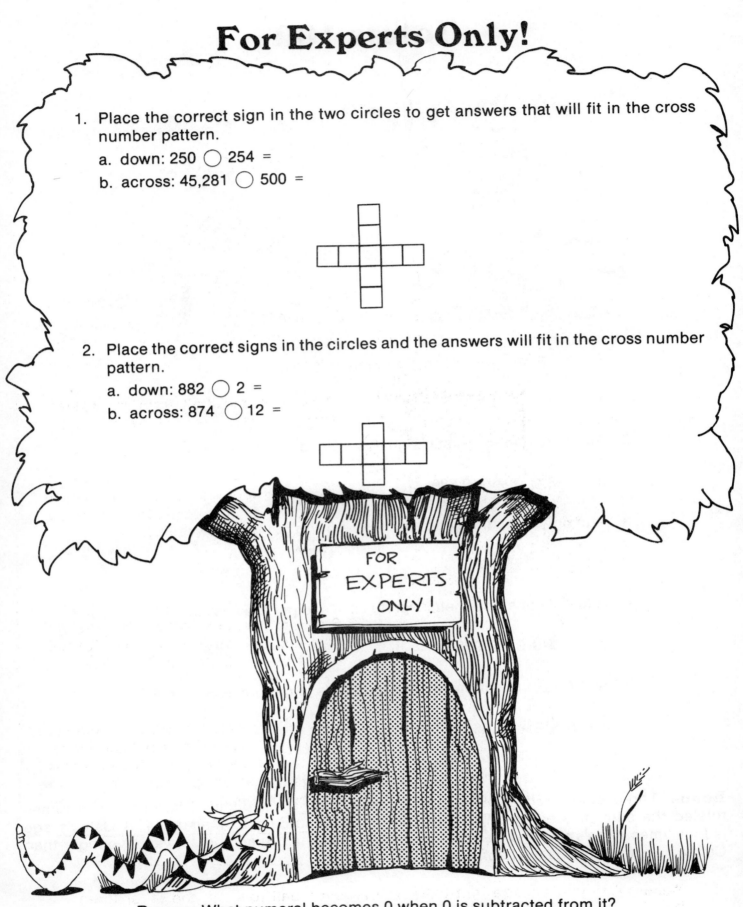

1.  Place the correct sign in the two circles to get answers that will fit in the cross number pattern.
    a.  down: 250 ◯ 254 =
    b.  across: 45,281 ◯ 500 =

2.  Place the correct signs in the circles and the answers will fit in the cross number pattern.
    a.  down: 882 ◯ 2 =
    b.  across: 874 ◯ 12 =

FOR EXPERTS ONLY!

**Bonus:** What numeral becomes 0 when 0 is subtracted from it?

Name _____

# Mystery Cross Out

1. Write down any five-digit number containing five different digits.
   Example: 98,651

2. Write the number backwards.
   Example: 15,689

3. Subtract the smaller number from the larger number.
   Example: 98,651 − 15,689 = 82,962

4. Cross out any digit from the answer except a zero. Example: 82,962

5. Add up the other digits. If the answer is more than one digit, add those digits.
   Example: 8 + 9 + 6 + 2 = 25 and 2 + 5 = 7

6. Subtract the sum from 9 and that will give you the mystery number crossed out in step 4. Example: 9 − 7 = 2

7. Now try some other five-digit numbers. When you have memorized the steps, have a friend write a number in secret and tell him you can figure out what number he crossed out without even looking.

Name_____

**Bonus:** Can you arrange four balls so that each ball touches the other three balls?

# Another Number Trick

1. Choose two numbers that have two digits each. Example: 59 and 34

2. Multiply the first number by two and divide the second number by 2.
   Example: 59 x 2 = 118 and 34 ÷ 2 = 17

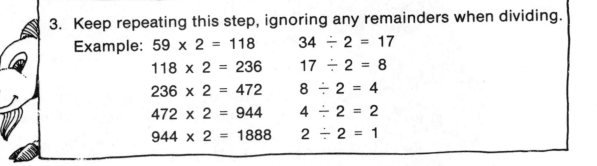

3. Keep repeating this step, ignoring any remainders when dividing.
   Example:  59 x 2 = 118        34 ÷ 2 = 17
            118 x 2 = 236        17 ÷ 2 = 8
            236 x 2 = 472        8 ÷ 2 = 4
            472 x 2 = 944        4 ÷ 2 = 2
            944 x 2 = 1888       2 ÷ 2 = 1

4. Look in the right column for any odd numbers in the total. Example: 17 and 1. Look across at the numbers in the opposite column of the odd numbers 17 and 1. Example: 118 and 1888. Then add these two numbers together. Example: 118 + 1888 = 2006.

5. Multiply the first two numbers you chose in step one. Example: 59 x 34 = 2006. You will get the same answer as in step 4. Try it again and again with other numbers. It always works!

**Bonus:** Can you find 1000, 100 and 10 hiding in the sentence found below?
My sister Cindy went out the EXIT.

Name _____

# Even Breaks

Divide the shape found below into four equal parts.

8

8

4

4

4

**Bonus:** Divide the shape found below into nine equal parts.

3

3

6

6

6

9

43

Name _____

# Painted Cubes

Pretend you have a cube 3" x 3" x 3". You paint the cube bright orange. Then you cut the cube into 1"cubes.

1. How many cubes would have no paint on them?

2. How many cubes would have one side painted orange?

3. How many cubes would have two sides painted orange?

4. How many cubes would have three sides painted orange?

5. How many cubes would have four sides painted orange?

**Bonus:** If you have a cube 4" x 4" x 4" and paint it purple and then cut it into 1" cubes, how many cubes would have no paint on them? One side painted? Two sides painted? Three sides painted?

Name _____

# Add a Stack of Digits

First decide by guessing which will total the most, 1 or 2? Then find the sum of each problem listed below to see if you were right.

|     | 1. | 123456789 |     | 2. | 987654321 |
|-----|----|-----------|-----|----|-----------|
|     |    | 12345678  |     |    | 87654321  |
|     |    | 1234567   |     |    | 7654321   |
|     |    | 123456    |     |    | 654321    |
|     |    | 12345     |     |    | 54321     |
|     |    | 1234      |     |    | 4321      |
|     |    | 123       |     |    | 321       |
|     |    | 12        |     |    | 21        |
|     |    | +1        |     |    | +1        |

**Bonus:** What is the total of all the numbers between 1 and 100?

Name _____

45

# An Easy One!

To discover a pattern, complete each problem found below.

$1 \times 9 + 2 =$

$12 \times 9 + 3 =$

$123 \times 9 + 4 =$

$1234 \times 9 + 5 =$

$12345 \times 9 + 6 =$

$123456 \times 9 + 7 =$

$1234567 \times 9 + 8 =$

$12345678 \times 9 + 9 =$

**Bonus:** Using three digits of equal numerical value, write two numerical equations that equal 30.

Example: $(5 \times 5) + 5 = 30$

Name _____

# Eight Is an Odd Number

Complete each problem found below to find out some interesting things about the number 8.

1 x 8 + 1 =

12 x 8 + 2 =

123 x 8 + 3 =

1234 x 8 + 4 =

12345 x 8 + 5 =

123456 x 8 + 6 =

1234567 x 8 + 7 =

12345678 x 8 + 8 =

123456789 x 8 + 9 =

**Bonus:** What number has the same product when multiplied by 8 and when multiplied by 9?

Name _____

# Let's Hear It for Number 8 Again!

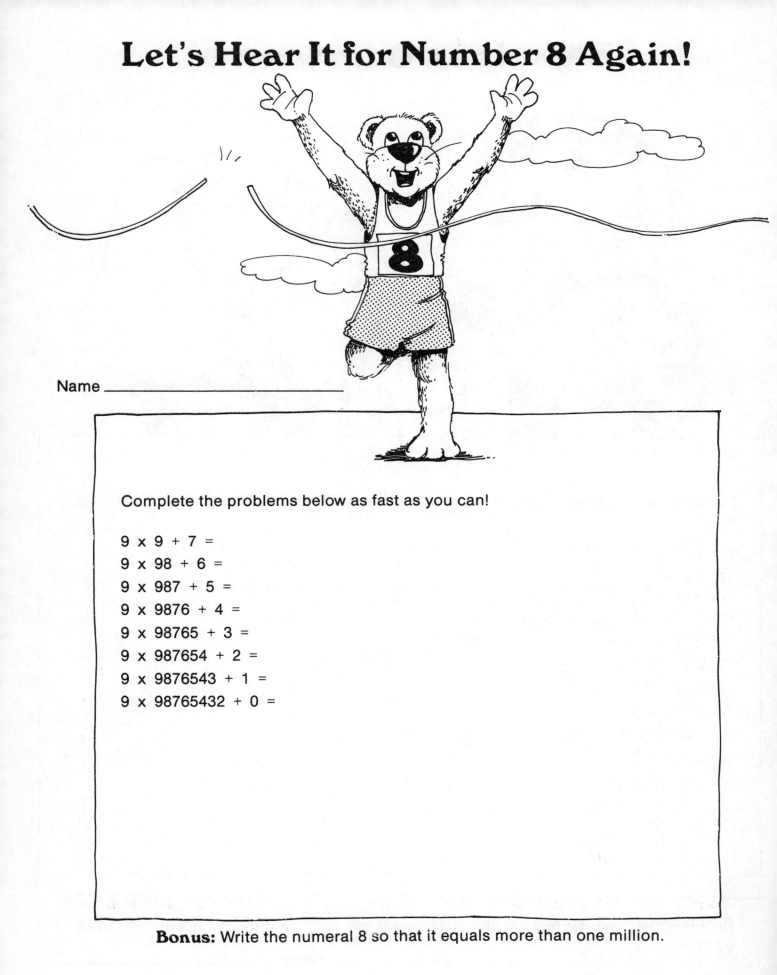

Name _____

Complete the problems below as fast as you can!

9 x 9 + 7 =

9 x 98 + 6 =

9 x 987 + 5 =

9 x 9876 + 4 =

9 x 98765 + 3 =

9 x 987654 + 2 =

9 x 9876543 + 1 =

9 x 98765432 + 0 =

**Bonus:** Write the numeral 8 so that it equals more than one million.

# Fibonacci

In about the year 1200 a mathematician, remembered now as Fibonacci, gained lasting fame by solving this problem. Can you solve the problem?

If we have one pair of rabbits and assuming the rabbit pair will produce another pair each month after the first, how many pairs of rabbits will we have at the end of one year?

January = 1 pair
February = 1 pair
March = 2 pairs
April =
May =
June =
July =
August =
September =
October =
November =
December =

**Bonus:** Write the pattern of numbers that gives the total number of rabbits. Extend the pattern until you reach the number 144.

Name _____

# More Fibonacci Numbers

Fibonacci's number pattern is 1, 1, 2, 3, 5, 8, 13, 21, 34, 55, 89, 144, 233, 377, 610, 987, etc. Each additional number is the total of the last two digits written. Use Fibonacci's number pattern to solve the problems below.

1. Write down any three consecutive numbers from the pattern. Square the middle number. Find the product of the other two numbers. How do they compare? Try this with other consecutive numbers. What pattern do you discover?

2. Add the first six numbers, skip the seventh number and compare your answer with the eighth number. Then add the first seven numbers, skip the eighth number and compare your answer with the ninth number. What pattern do you discover?

**Bonus:** Find a pattern of your own using the Fibonacci number pattern.

Name _____

# Dot and Line Problems

1. Put nine dots on your paper so that there are five rows containing three dots.

2. Put ten dots in five rows with four dots in each row.

**Bonus:** Show another solution for problem 1.

Name _____

# You Pick the Numbers

Choose any one-digit number to be added to the problems below. Write it in the blank and then add the numbers. Repeat until you have completed all four problems. Do you see a pattern?

1. 1 2 3, 4 5 6, 7 8 9
   9 8 7, 6 5 4, 3 2 1
   1 2 3, 4 5 6, 7 8 9
   9 8 7, 6 5 4, 3 2 1
   _____ + ☐

2. 1 2 3, 4 5 6, 7 8 9
   9 8 7, 6 5 4, 3 2 1
   1 2 3, 4 5 6, 7 8 9
   9 8 7, 6 5 4, 3 2 1
   _____ + ☐

3. 1 2 3, 4 5 6, 7 8 9
   9 8 7, 6 5 4, 3 2 1
   1 2 3, 4 5 6, 7 8 9
   9 8 7, 6 5 4, 3 2 1
   _____ + ☐

4. 1 2 3, 4 5 6, 7 8 9
   9 8 7, 6 5 4, 3 2 1
   1 2 3, 4 5 6, 7 8 9
   9 8 7, 6 5 4, 3 2 1
   _____ + ☐

**Bonus:** If you subtract the mystery number from both 100 and 20, one answer will be 6 times larger than the other answer. What is the mystery number?

Name _____

# Do You Believe It?

Complete both of the multiplication problems found below. Time yourself on the first problem. Then use the pattern you discovered in problem 1 to help you do problem 2. Time yourself on problem 2 also.

1.   7 6, 9 2 3
   x 6 8, 2 7 5

2.   1 4 2, 8 5 7
   x 3 2 6, 4 5 1

**Bonus:** Charlie is twice as old as Eric was when Charlie was as old as Eric is now. How old is each man?

Name _____

# Mathematical Bogglers

1. Draw only three lines to divide the circle into eight sections.

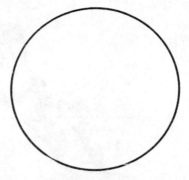

2. Add five lines to the lines below to make nine.

| | | | | | |

3. Remove two lines to leave two squares.

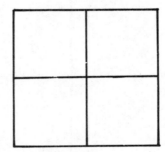

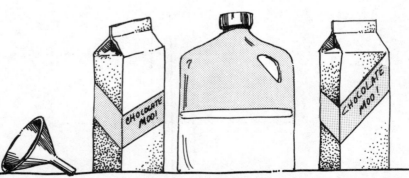

**Bonus:** Mrs. Jones was cleaning out her refrigerator. She found a quart of chocolate milk half full, and she poured it into a gallon carton of white milk that was half empty. Then she found another quart of chocolate milk that was only one-quarter full. She poured that into the same gallon container. She shook the milk up and put it back in the refrigerator. What fractional part of the milk was chocolate?

Name _____

# All in All

Can you arrange the digits 1, 2, 3 and 4 so that each row, each column and each diagonal contains all four digits? The first row is filled in for you.

| 1 | 2 | 3 | 4 |
|---|---|---|---|
|   |   |   |   |
|   |   |   |   |
|   |   |   |   |

**Bonus:** Can you arrange the digits 1, 2, 3, 4 and 5 so that each row, each column and each diagonal contains all five digits?

| | | | | |
|---|---|---|---|---|
|   |   |   |   |   |
|   |   |   |   |   |
|   |   |   |   |   |
|   |   |   |   |   |

Name _____

# Answer Key

## Number Patterns Page 1
1. 24 (add 5, subtract 2, repeat)
2. 92 (multiply by 2, add 4, repeat)
3. 888 (multiply by 3, add 2, repeat)
4. 342 (multiply by 5, add 7, repeat)
5. 43 (add 1, add 2, add 3, etc.)
6. 32 (add 7, add 6, add 5, etc.)
Bonus: 74,070 (add 66, 666, 6666, etc.)

## Associations Page 2
1. 1 (first number is 5 times second number)
2. 130 (the second number is the first number plus 20)
3. 12 (the second number equals the sum of the first digits)
4. 18 (the second number is 1½ times the first number)
5. 18 (the second number is the first and last digits of the first number, reversed and middle digit dropped)
Bonus: The second number is the first number upside down.

## A Difficult Arrangement Page 3
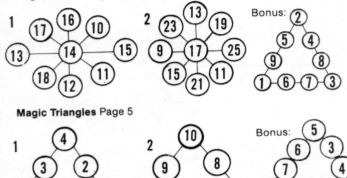
Bonus: 3
7
5-9-1-6-2
4
8

## Magic Circles Page 4

## Magic Triangles Page 5
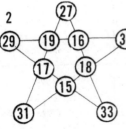

## Magic Stars Page 6
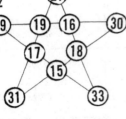

## Magic Squares Page 7
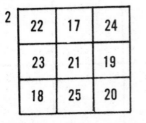
Bonus: 196

## Magic Square Formula Page 8

| 99 | 89 | 103 |
|----|----|-----|
| 101 | 97 | 93 |
| 91 | 105 | 95 |

Bonus: $10 each, if one of the mothers is the daughter of the other mother. Example: grandmother, mother (mother and daughter) and daughter.

## I See Spots Page 9
1. 46      5. 0
2. 7       6. 0
3. 6       7. 0
4. 61      8. 10

## I See Spots (cont'd.) Page 10
9. 32      12. 18      15. 33
10. 10     13. 77      16. 5
11. 0      14. 17      17. 10

## Cut the Pies Page 11

Bonus: 197 (100 divided by ½ = 200, + 16 = 216, - 19 = 197)

## Ring Just Three Page 12
2. Mystery sum is 15.

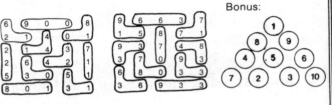

## Fractions Page 13
1. 7/98     4. 100         Bonus: 792
2. 98/7     5. 108 days
3. 102

## More Fractions Page 14
1. 132 days
2. Not if he had an uneven number of eggs. Example: If he had 7 eggs, he sold half his eggs (3½) plus ½ egg, totals 4 eggs.
3. c. (Odds are not affected by previous children. There is always a 50% chance of having a girl.)
Bonus: 6 (1/3 of 12 = 4 and ½ of 1/3 = 1/6 of 12 or 2. 4 + 2 = 6.)

## A Question of Time Page 15
1. 500 minutes or 8 and 1/3 hours
2. 2 minutes and 15 seconds (each slice has two sides: a1, a2, b1, b2, c1, c2). Begin by toasting a1 and b1 for 45 seconds. Then toast a2 and c1 for 45 seconds. Last toast b2 and c2 for an additional 45 seconds.
3. 7:40
4. 90 times
Bonus: Roberta will be late.

## Money Problems Page 16
1. 1 quarter, 2 nickels and 3 pennies
2. 1 twenty, 2 tens, 3 fives, 1 one, 1 half dollar, 1 quarter, 2 dimes, 1 nickel and 3 pennies

3. 4 dozen eggs = $2, 6 dozen apples = $1.80
Bonus: 1 fifty dollar bill, 1 five dollar bill and 2 two dollar bills = $59

### More Money Problems Page 17
1. gumdrops = 3¢, lollipops = 2¢ and peppermint patties = 4¢
2. less than, 50 weeks total
3. Monday $20, Tuesday $40 and Wednesday $10
Bonus: 5 quarters, 20 dimes, 25 nickels and 50 pennies or 1 half dollar, 39 dimes and 60 pennies

### Cross All Ways Page 18

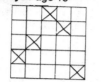
Bonus:
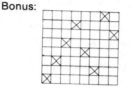

### Pure Magic Squares Page 19

1
| 6 | 1 | 8 |
|---|---|---|
| 7 | 5 | 3 |
| 2 | 9 | 4 |

2
| 12 | 7 | 14 |
|----|----|----|
| 13 | 11 | 9 |
| 8 | 15 | 10 |

Bonus: A pound of feathers weighs more than a pound of gold. Most things have 16 ounces in a pound; however, gold is measured in troy weight which is 12 ounces.

### More Pure Magic Squares Page 20

1
| 27 | 20 | 25 |
|----|----|----|
| 22 | 24 | 26 |
| 23 | 28 | 21 |

2
| 11 | 1 | 15 |
|----|----|----|
| 13 | 9 | 5 |
| 3 | 17 | 7 |

3
| 20 | 10 | 24 |
|----|----|----|
| 22 | 18 | 14 |
| 12 | 26 | 16 |

Bonus:
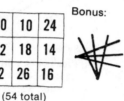

(54 total)

### Mathematical Codes Page 21

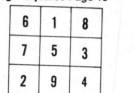

### Another Mathematical Code Page 22
0 = g, 1 = f, 2 = a, 3 = e, 4 = b, 5 = d

### Word Problems Page 23
1. Nannette, 30; Jay, 40; Brad, 10
2. 163
3. Martha, 830; Joe, 209; Wally, 415
4. Zero, chickens don't talk.
Bonus: 275 feet

### More Word Problems Page 24
1. 5 and 7 are reversed.
2. one stack
3. 1
4. 0
5. c. (Previous rolls do not affect the odds of a new roll.)
Bonus: 24 orange, 12 green, 11 blue, 19 red

### Mathematical Sentences Page 25
1. E = 1, R =2, N =3, O =4, Y = 5, P = 7, S = 8, A = 9, T = 0
2. O = 1, L = 2, N = 3, M = 5, U = 6, I = 7, P = 8, S = 9, W = 0
3. O = 0, I = 1, P = 2, D = 3, F = 4, E = 5, S = 6, N = 7, H = 8, L = 9
Bonus: 5 words and 1 name: she = 3:45, Lee = 3:37, see = 3:35, lie = 3:17, hoe = 3:04, lei = 1:37

### It Is Possible Page 26
1. Turn the paper upside down and circle the digits 9, 9 and 8.
2. Circle the digits 1, 4 and 6.
Bonus: The difference is 20 (2 x 22 = 44) while (2 x 2) + 20 = 24

### Where's the Sign? Page 27
1. 789 - 36 = 753
2. 724 + 91 = 815
3. 6324 x 3 = 18,972
4. 5091 + 89 = 5180
5. 568 x 34 = 19,312
6. 7070 ÷ 7 = 1010
7. 934 x 463 = 432,442
8. 7043 - 84 = 6959
9. 6021 x 3 = 18,063
10. 4521 - 31 = 4490

Bonus: Put #4 on #1, #6 on #9, #8 on #3, #2 on #5 and #10 on #7.

### Signing Off Page 28
1. 701 x 52 = 36,452
2. 8934 ÷ 6 = 1489
3. 4365 x 3 = 13,095
4. 1452 x 20 = 29,040
5. 12,342 ÷ 6 = 2057
6. 58205 ÷ 5 = 1164
Bonus: 1 + 2 + 3 = 1 x 2 x 3

### Double Trouble Page 29
1. 72 + 80 = 152
2. 93 ÷ 3 = 31
3. 95 - 90 = 5
4. 810 - 11 = 799
5. 894 ÷ 6 = 149    Bonus: 19
6. 9783 + 20 = 9803

### Slip, Please Page 30
First—6,3; Second—4,5; Third—5,7; Fourth—0,8; Fifth—9,2
Bonus: 81

### Think First Page 31
1. 1001
2. 12,944
3. 9,000,045
4. 8585
5. 1,100,001
6. 7266

Bonus: 1 (After that you are not subtracting from 1000.)

### Big Fives Page 32
1. $55 + 5 + 5 = 65$
2. $55 + \frac{55}{5} = 66$
3. $55 + \frac{5}{5} + \frac{5}{5} = 57$
4. $555 \times 55 = 30,525$
5. $555,555 \div 5 = 10,101$
6. $\frac{555}{5} = 111$

Bonus: Because its capital is always Dublin (doubling).

### Lucky 7's Page 33
1. $7 \times \frac{77}{77} = 7$
2. $7 + \frac{77}{77} - \frac{7}{7} = 7$
3. $777 \times 77 = 59,829$
4. 777 - 77 = 700
5. 7777 ÷ 77 = 101
6. 142

Bonus: Seven becomes EVEN if its first letter (head) is chopped off.

### Consecutive Numbers Page 34
1. 1, 2, 3
2. 89, 91, 93
3. 11, 13, 15, 17, 19
4. 60, 62, 64, 66, 68
5. Divide the total of the digits by the number of consecutive digits and that will equal the middle consecutive digit.

Bonus: 5, 765 x 55 = 42,075 (Did you assume because the digit 5 was given once in the problem that it wouldn't be the mystery number?)

### What Number? Page 35
1. 8
2. $\frac{88}{8} = 11$
3. 24
4. 49
5. 1, 1

Bonus: 1 hour and 12 minutes (Eric would do half the job in one hour. John would do one-third the job in one hour. Then they would have ⅙ of the work left which together they could do in ⅕ of an hour or 12 minutes.)

**Products** Page 36
1. 47 x 3 = 141
2. 15 x 39 = 585
3. 1 x 61 = 61
4. 66
5. 88
6. 1, 3, 9
7. 13, 15, 17

Bonus: A butcher weighs meat. (His body weight cannot be determined with the information given.)

**Just a Speck** Page 37
1. Add a decimal point in front of the digit 9.
2. when it is 6:00
3. 2 ÷ 87 = .0229885
4. 5 9 1
   7
   3

Bonus: There are no grains of sand in a hole.

**Puzzle Picture** Page 38
1. 26
2. 8
3. 0
4. 4
5. 2
6. 47
7. 26

**Totals 100** Page 39
1. 111 - 11 = 100
2. 333 x 333 = 110,889
3. 555 - 55 = 500
4. 999 + 999 = 1998
5. 8888 + 8 = 8896

Bonus: Alice 4, Becky 10, Cathy 16

**For Experts Only!** Page 40
1. a. 250 x 254 = 63,500
   b. 45,281 ÷ 500 = 90.562
2. a. 882 ÷ 2 = 441
   b. 874 x 12 = 10,488

Bonus: Zero or 8. Take away the top circle leaving a circle on the bottom.

**Mystery Cross Out** Page 41
Bonus: Put three balls flat on the floor touching in a triangular position. Rest the fourth ball on top of the other three balls in the center so it touches all of the other balls.

**Another Number Trick** Page 42
Bonus: The Roman numerals: M = 1000; C = 100 and X = 10 are hidden in the sentence.

**Even Breaks** Page 43

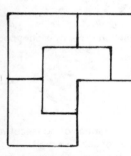

Bonus:

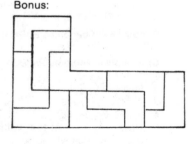

**Painted Cubes** Page 44
1. 1, 2. 6, 3. 12, 4. 8, 5. 0
Bonus: 0 = 4, 1 = 24, 2 = 28, 3 = 8

**Add a Stack of Digits** Page 45
Both equal 1,083,676,269.
Bonus: 5050

**An Easy One!** Page 46
11; 111; 1111; 11,111; 111,111; 1,111,111; 11,111,111; 111,111,111
Bonus: 33 - 3 = 30 and 10 + 10 + 10 = 30

**Eight Is an Odd Number** Page 47
9; 98; 987; 9876; 98,765; 987,654; 9,876,543; 98,765,432; 987,654,321
Bonus: 0

**Let's Hear It for Number 8 Again!** Page 48
88; 888; 8888; 88,888; 888,888; 8,888,888; 88,888,888; 888,888,888
Bonus: Turn it on its side so it is infinity.

**Fibonacci** Page 49
According to Fibonacci: January 1 = 1 pair; February 1 = 1 pair; March 1 = 2 pairs; April 1 = 3 pairs; May 1 = 5 pairs; June 1 = 8 pairs; July 1 = 13 pairs; August 1 = 21 pairs; September 1 = 34 pairs; October 1 = 55 pairs; November 1 = 89 pairs; December 1 = 144 pairs.
Bonus: 1, 1, 2, 3, 5, 8, 13, 21, 34, etc. The total of two consecutive numbers equals the third number, etc.

**More Fibonacci Numbers** Page 50
1. The product of the first and last number is always one less than the square of the second number.
2. The total of any number of consecutive numbers is one less than the number once removed from the last number added. Example: 1 + 1 + 2 = 1 less than 5 (the number once removed from 2).

**Dot and Line Problems** Page 51

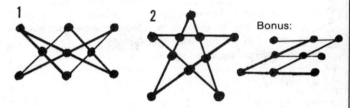

1          2          Bonus:

**You Pick the Number** Page 52
All the numbers in the answer will be the same except for the last number, which will be the number you added.
Bonus: 4

**Do You Believe It?** Page 53

```
1.   7 6,9 2 3
   x 6 8,2 7 5
   _____
     3 8 4 6 1 5
     5 3 8 4 6 1
     1 5 3 8 4 6
     6 1 5 3 8 4
 +   4 6 1 5 3 8
   _____
   5,2 5 1,9 1 7,8 2 5
```

```
2.   1 4 2,8 5 7
   x 3 2 6,4 5 1
   _____
     1 4 2 8 5 7
     7 1 4 2 8 5
     5 7 1 4 2 8
     8 5 7 1 4 2
     2 8 5 7 1 4
 +   4 2 8 5 7 1
   _____
   4 6,6 3 5,8 1 0,5 0 7
```

Bonus: Charlie is 24; Eric is 18.

**Mathematical Bogglers** Page 54
1.

2. N I N E
3.

Bonus: ³/₁₁

**All in All** Page 55

| 1 | 2 | 3 | 4 |
|---|---|---|---|
| 4 | 3 | 2 | 1 |
| 2 | 1 | 4 | 3 |
| 3 | 4 | 1 | 2 |

Bonus:

| 4 | 1 | 3 | 5 | 2 |
|---|---|---|---|---|
| 3 | 5 | 2 | 4 | 1 |
| 2 | 4 | 1 | 3 | 5 |
| 1 | 3 | 5 | 2 | 4 |
| 5 | 2 | 4 | 1 | 3 |

# Bonus Award Certificate

TO _____

_____

FROM _____

_____

# Mathematical Genius Award

To _____

From _____

61 X 5 = 305

# Numbers Expert

To _____

From _____

1 52 = 3645

# Math Whiz Kid

To _____

_____

From _____

_____

# Award Certificate

To _____

_____

From _____

_____

# Extra Effort Award

To _____

From _____